I Am A Big

Thai Male

Prostitute

I Am A Big Thai Male Prostitute
A Humorous Confession

Phlap Apirak

The Hermit Kingdom Press
Cheltenham ◆ Seoul ◆ Bangalore ◆ Cebu

I AM A BIG THAI MALE PROSTITUTE:
A HUMOROUS CONFESSION

Copyright © 2005 by Phlap Apirak

ISBN 1-59689-039-8 (paperback)
ISBN 1-59689-040-1 (Adobe ebook)

Write-To Address:

The Hermit Kingdom Press
3741 Walnut Street, Suite 407
Philadelphia, PA 19104
United States of America

Info@TheHermitKingdomPress.com

★ ★ ★ ★

Hermit Kingdom
12 South Bridge, Suite 370
Edinburgh, EH1 1DD
Scotland

http://www.TheHermitKingdomPress.com

"He sees death in the prostitutes who have witnessed the death of honor, and daily multiply the death of love, who bleed away their own lives 50 times a day beneath the relentless stabbings of countless conjugations."

Ed McBain

Contents

for me, myself, and I

The Confession

Yeah, you are right. You have heard about us. We exist. We are a group of highly trained, physically well-endowed individuals with one purpose in life. Yeah, that's right. We exist here to provide services – services of the carnal kind.

Of course, the services are for hire. People pay good money for our services. For, depravity costs money. There are all kinds of opportunities in the world of sin for people like us – like me.

Yeah, you are probably right. God did not give us good endowments of the physical kind to corrupt His beautiful world with. But what do we care? We are male prostitutes. We have no morals. We have no qualms. We just want to make money. We want to capitalize on sin and human depravity.

And I am the best of them, you see. I am the best endowed as far as I can see. I like to brag and brag about my big physical endowment. I can't help but feel the urge to show it off at every opportunity.

But even a moral degenerate like me have principles. No, not principles of the moral kind. Rather, principles guided by dollars and cents. That's the sense that keeps me in my pants.

But I have found a way to show it off and make money doing it. You see my principles coupled with my intelligence will make me a whole bucketful of money, you see.

Yeah, you may look down on me, but I will be rich and make a lot of money. I will make far more money doing the degenerate thing in a one year period than you can ever hope to make in a 10 year period busting your butt at an honest job.

Yeah, you have your Christian values, but I have my principles based on money and degeneration.

After all, isn't life all about gambling? I have found a way to gamble on life and make loads of money doing it. So, what's up with that?

Yeah, I am a Thai male prostitute. I am a big Thai male prostitute. And you know what is big? Yeah, you know.

I have the raw materials and I have found a way to make a lot of money capitalizing on it.

People pay a lot of money for my services of the carnal, degenerate kind.

Yeah, you are probably right. I should be ashamed of myself for capitalizing on degeneration and sinful nature of humanity.

Maybe deep inside, in the hidden corners of my inner being, I may feel guilty. Maybe the guilt will come and haunt me in the future.

But I have to confess that for now, I feel no guilt. Yeah, you heard me. I feel no guilt. I feel no remorse.

I am having too much fun, showing off my big equipment and making a lot of money through my degeneration enterprise.

There is a lot of money in sin. Isn't the forbidden fruit the most tasty? Just ask Adam and Eve!

Yeah, I am a big Thai male prostitute. My thingy is big and I am darned proud of my thingy. Yeah, you heard me. I am darned proud.

I have found a way to show it off and make a lot of money with it. I am a big Thai male prostitute and I am proud of it. That is my confession.

Hmmm. That sounds almost musical – maybe I'll make a song out of it. Do you think hip-hop would work? Maybe I can hip-hop to those words in a distinctive Thai hip-hop style. I can hip-hop in Thai and English. Wouldn't that be cool?

Just call me the Grandmaster Biggy Thingy Thai. Yeah, that's the ticket. Grandmaster Biggy Thingy Thai.

Yeah, let's try this thing. I will try to hip-hop my confession in English. Here it goes.

I am the Grandmaster Biggy Thingy Thai. Just call me the

Grandmaster Biggy Thingy Thai. Yeah! Biggy Thingy Thai, Grandmaster I am.

I like to show of my biggy thingy. Yeah! Biggy thingy of mine for you to see. Biggy thingy that God gave me. Yeah, He probably gave me the biggy thing for marriage. But Baptist pastor, don't tell me what to do with my biggy thingy. God don't tell me what to do with my biggy thingy. You may have given it to me but it's mine now. Yeah! And I'll do with my biggy thingy whatever thingy I want.

I will show off my biggy thingy, yeah! To make me rich, I will show off my biggy thingy. Come see my biggy thingy, yeah! Touch my biggy thingy, yeah! Go on, touch my biggy thingy, yeah!

Just remember to pay your hard earned money for my biggy thingy, yeah! I am the Grandmaster Biggy Thingy Thai. Yeah! I am proud to be the Grandmaster Biggy Thingy Thai. And I will make enough money to buy God Himself.

How does that sound? Does it sound like I have the makings of a hip-hop gold platinum?

I know my big endowment will take me places. I will travel the world and show off my biggy thingy. I will use my big endowment for degenerate gain.

Move aside God. There is a new grandmaster in town. Yeah, you heard me. I am the Grandmaster Biggy Thingy Thai.

The Training

Yeah, we have to be trained – we prostitutes, I mean. Yeah, I do have the biggy thingy, but I still have to be trained in the art of prostitution. Here, I will share some of my secret with you. Yeah, you heard me.

Many people think that being a male prostitute is all about sexually pleasuring women. Nothing can be so far from the truth. Male prostitution is a business. And like all business, male prostitution is meant to make money, lots of it.

I am not saying that pleasuring women is not a part of the male prostitution game. It certainly is a part of it. But it is not the most important part of being a male prostitute. You can't make a lot of money by being good at pleasuring women. How many women can you pleasure?

Let's consider the business side of things. Let's say that a male prostitute is paid per pleasure service that he provides a woman at the going prostitute rate, there is no way that I can become rich.

Just think. How many really wealthy prostitutes do you know? To become rich being a prostitute, it's important to get training.

The training that I am talking about is not about the sexual kind. I am talking about training in psychological manipulation and social deception. That's where the money is. Before I talk about how the training culminates in riches, I will tell you about the training.

Yeah, you can get some specialized training in psychology and sociology at Harvard and apply the theory to being an effective male prostitute. And some prostitutes take the route of education. It helps them develop the psychological edge that can be used to capitalize on depravity cash.

An added side benefit of getting a Harvard education is that you become more sellable. Yeah, there is a market for Ivy League prostitutes. Some people will pay extra cash for conversation. Human beings often have more need of intimacy and communication than they do in the sexual area. That's just human nature.

Although Harvard education would help, I prefer the training under one or a few experts.

Just like any business, male prostitution requires learning the trade. For someone like me who wants to make lots of money from male prostitution, I have to become an expert particularly in the area of psychological manipulation and social deception. That's where all the money is. Yeah, you heard me.

I will tell you about my training. I learned under a couple of masters, actively. I learned psychological manipulation from an Eastern European doctor. He boasted of having royal ties. I didn't even know that Eastern Europe had royalty. We in Thailand just think of Eastern Europeans as ex-communists who were able to throw off the oppressive yolk of oppression. I bet he was one of the oppressors during the communist regime days.

But his manipulative mind served me well because I wanted to be trained in the art of psychological manipulation.

I have a biggy thingy. I was just born with it. But psychological manipulation has to be learned. I was a wide-eyed, positive, and naïve child filled with hope and love of humanity. You can't get anywhere in the world with that kind of an attitude. Only the ruthless survive and thrive, right? That's the first thing that Dr. Eastern Europe taught me.

Yeah, the first thing that Dr. Eastern Europe taught me was to be ruthless. He said that there is no glory in honor but there is money in immoral ruthlessness.

At first, I cringed to hear Dr. Eastern Europe's depraved life philosophy laid bare before me. But then I got used to it as he bombarded me with the idea of ruthlessness and its profitability for the personal pocket.

Soon enough, the idea of personal wealth made his unscrupulous ideas of immoral ruthlessness attractive to me. What's the point of being moral if one remains poor, right? In this world, only money speaks? Money speaks, the world listens. A moral man speaks, no one listens.

Dr. Eastern Europe's arguments made sense to me. I wanted to be wealthy and I came to realize he was the perfect trainer for psychological manipulation.

Dr. Eastern Europe taught that in being immorally ruthless, one has to learn to betray anything and everyone. What counts is you, yourself, and you, Dr. Eastern Europe said. Friendships don't matter. Family honor doesn't matter. Respecting other humans don't matter. To become wealthy, one has to disentangle oneself from all that is decent and respectful in human relationships. You just have to care about yourself and your goal of making money.

Slowly, Dr. Eastern Europe helped me to see that for personal gain, it was okay to betray one's closest friends. I came to feel comfortable with the idea of humiliating my closest family members without remorse or regret in order to obtain personal wealth. That went double for other family members. My heart was hardened to the extent that I could keep my eyes wide open and keep smiling as I screwed over other people's mothers and fathers. I took pride in humiliating other people's wives and husbands. Dr. Eastern Europe made me an immoral, ruthless man. I became a hardened man – I was no longer a softy with a boyish innocence.

It became clear to me how Eastern European communist regime leaders kept normal Eastern Europe under control during communist oppression. It worked for them, so it would work for me.

In my training in psychological manipulation, the second thing that Dr. Eastern Europe taught me was the artifice of emotional manipulation. Dr. Eastern Europe said that if a person practices immoral emotional manipulation effectively, he will become wealthy beyond his wildest dreams.

In my capacity as a male prostitute, important emotional manipulation was learning to manipulate the emotion of a woman. Dr. Eastern Europe told me that it is important to learn to hook a woman – even a decent woman – and then break her down and even humiliate her in a clever way. True brilliance, Dr. Eastern Europe told me, was in being able to make a woman feel like nothing and then manipulate her to look to you to build her up.

True brilliant master of emotional manipulation can make the woman attached to him even as he humiliates her worse than he would his dog.

I was no hater of women so this kind of misogynous talk made me uncomfortable at first. But Dr. Eastern Europe put me at ease quickly enough.

Dr. Eastern Europe taught me a few tricks to manipulating women emotionally in an effective way to bond her to you – or rather, to enslave her under your influence.

The most important rule, Dr. Eastern Europe told me, is to break her down and make her feel worthless.

At first, I thought that it didn't make sense. Why would anyone be bonded to you if you are mean to them and make them feel worthless? If you were successful, wouldn't she just go out there and commit suicide?

Dr. Eastern Europe told me that breaking her down and making her feel worthless is only the one step in the process. Dr. Eastern Europe encouraged me to think in terms of enslaving the woman.

Think about slavery, he said. Black slaves were not kept down by showing tender-loving-care. Black slaves were kept down under white slave owners by ruthlessness. Blacks were made to feel worthless about themselves. This prevented black slaves from rising up against white slave owners. Although there might have been hundreds of black slaves under a few white slave owners, these black slave owners were made to feel that they did not have worth and they could not rise up against the few. It was psychological.

Dr. Eastern Europe said that enslaving a woman under your influence is the same thing. Yeah, it's misogynous and encourages the philosophical outlook of women as weak and under male sexual power, but who cares about morals when there was money to be made.

Dr. Eastern Europe explained to me that if I mastered the technique of psychological manipulation in enslaving a woman, then I would become a rich man.

I was, of course, all ears after that. Dr. Eastern Europe showed me how to break a woman down and enslave her.

Dr. Eastern Europe said that the first thing that I had to do is win the woman's trust. Be nice to her and try to seem like a good guy. She will think that she can put her trust in you and put her trust in you. Psychologically, this is her first step to capitulation.

I thought to myself: Isn't giving oneself up a part of the loving process? It's the mutual giving up of self that makes love possible, no?

Dr. Eastern Europe said that I was right. But I wasn't like most normal people. I was to learn psychological manipulation to enslave women for financial gain. Most people think of love as a nice thing that they want to experience. I was to think of love as a commodity, a method to use to enslave women and take their money. It was a business enterprise for me and I had to get that quickly into my mind.

It was hard to deprogram myself with all the positive elements that I was used to and reprogram myself with negative thinking. But with the help of

32

Dr. Eastern Europe, I slowly felt myself becoming rewired into a mean-lean-driving machine.

Yeah, it was true. The women who meet me will be completely ruined in the love department, Dr. Eastern Europe said. But I was to remain resolute in my ruthlessness, Dr. Eastern Europe emphasized. That is the only way to make lots of money.

Money, money, and more money! I repeated over and over again and tried to desensitize myself. I was going to get rid of my God-given conscience. It was worth it for all the money that was coming my way.

After all, is financial success possible without ruining some people along the way? Dr. Eastern Europe was very convincing.

Yeah, I was to win the trust of the women that I prey upon in order to enslave them to myself. Dr. Eastern Europe said that once I have won the trust of the woman prey and that I was sure of it, I must begin the process of psychological manipulation in earnest.

After she gives herself to you, Dr. Eastern Europe said, start the psychological manipulation program with few negative comments about her. They shouldn't be too overtly negative but rather quite subtle.

This would transition her into the phase of doubt. She will begin to doubt herself. She will begin to feel bad about herself. This is crucial, Dr. Eastern Europe said, to enslaving her.

If she feels good about herself, she cannot be easily manipulated. When she is strong, she cannot be enslaved. It is when she feels weak, you can enslave her. It is when she feels a lack of self-confidence that you can manipulate her into doing what you want her to do.

Dr. Eastern Europe said that the subtle comments to make her unsure of herself should be followed by an active program to help her hate herself.

Dr. Eastern Europe told me what I needed to do. I was to start making more overtly critical and negative comments about her. For instance, I could say that she looks fat. Or, I can say that her ears are ugly.

Negative comments like these will start eating away at her. She will be mad at you at first. But then, with passage of time, she will become more mad at herself. She will begin to ask herself if the statements are true. Even if the statements are not true, she will begin to believe in them. She will begin to hate herself. She will come to believe in the statement as the absolute truth, like the statement that the earth is round.

Dr. Eastern Europe explained that this is one of the mysteries of women's psyche. As established as a woman is, as accomplished as she is, as intelligent as a she is, she will – by the virtue of being a woman – come to believe in the negative statements about her. She will not only come to believe in them but will hate herself for it. This is the mystery that is woman, Dr. Eastern Europe said.

Dr. Eastern Europe said that it is crucial that the negative comments, particularly overtly negative comments, are not made before the woman has declared her affection for you. When a woman says that she loves you, she has given herself up. It doesn't matter how intelligent, how powerful, how wealthy a woman is. When a woman says she loves you, she has made herself completely vulnerable. This is where men are different. Men are not like that.

Of course, most women don't expect to be psychologically manipulated when they give themselves up. And there are enough nice guys out there who will not misuse women's emotions or feelings. But Dr. Eastern Europe reminded me that for those of enterprise to make money through depravity, what psychological damage will be wrought on a woman should be of no concern. What's important is that you make money.

Think about you, you, you!

Dr. Eastern Europe said that you should not stop with overtly negative comments. Dr. Eastern Europe said that it's important to get the woman to do degrading things. The more respectable a woman is, the more important it is to get her to do degrading things. This is an important part of psychological manipulation to enslave her under your influence.

It should be easier to get her to do degrading things and self-humiliating things, if you have made her hate herself and insecure about herself, Dr. Eastern Europe said with an evil smile on his face. I still see that smile and can hear the Eastern European laugh, which is his trade mark.

Dr. Eastern Europe's sinister laughter is certainly one for the movies. It is creepy as hell and has a touch of evil that is strategic and intelligent. Evil intelligence. I still feel shivers up and down my spine when I think about it. I try to be evil but he is evil. Maybe it's years of Communism that conditioned him to be that way. After all, he probably participated in oppressing normal people in a Communist regime as an elite in the Communist structure.

With that sinister laughter, Dr. Eastern Europe explained to me what kind of things I can do to make her my psychological slave.

Dr. Eastern Europe said that the simplest thing that I can do to make her feel self-degradation and humiliation is to get her to beg for sex. Yeah, beg for sex.

Dr. Eastern Europe explained that begging for sex is a dirty act. Especially when a woman thinks about it afterwards, she will feel a sense of humiliation and degradation. In the actual sexual context as things happen, it may not seem so degrading because everything is happening so quickly. But afterwards, that's when the woman will realize what she has done. The sense of degradation, humiliation, and guilt will take her one step closer to making her your slave – sex slave.

The key, Dr. Eastern Europe said, is to get her to hate herself and feel lack of self-worth. Then, she will belong to you as a slave forever.

Getting her to beg for sex may not always be easy, Dr. Eastern Europe explained. That is why he's there – to teach how to do it. Dr. Eastern Europe is experienced in the techniques of psychological manipulation, I came to realize quickly. As a person who wanted to make money through degeneration and sin, I knew that Dr. Eastern Europe was the right person to teach me how to do it all.

Dr. Eastern Europe explained that the easiest way to get a woman to beg for sex is in the context of sexual acts. For instance, when you are both naked and understand that you are about to have sex, give the woman foreplay without intercourse. When she is expecting the intercourse, instead of smoothly transitioning into the sexual intercourse, tell her to beg for sex. She may be taken aback at first and look at you strangely. Just ignore her look. Disregard her feelings. Just focus on the fact that you are trying to make her into your sex slave.

If she hesitates, firmly repeat again that she should beg for sex. Soon, she will cave in and ask for sex. She may ask quietly and in a coy manner. She may be shy about it. Don't let her off easy. Get her to beg for sex more loudly. It is best when you get her to beg for sex again and again. Tell her that you didn't quite hear her. Tell her to repeat it again. Ask her in a mocking way: Do you really want me to give it to you? Taunt her after she has asked for sex. Make her feel degradation and humiliation. This is more important for later, when she will have a chance to reflect on her own begging for sex.

Dr. Eastern Europe said that psychological manipulation was precisely that. It was meant to manipulate the individual. It wasn't easy. That is why it's called psychological manipulation. It's not supposed to be nice or kind. The end result is to enslave her sexually to you.

And of course, there is the important purpose. You are trying to become rich out of it all.

At first, I had doubts about the possibility of getting a woman to beg for sex, especially if she is a respectable woman.

Dr. Eastern Europe told me this and I remember it clear as day to this day. Dr. Eastern Europe said: Read the Bible. Huh? Yeah, you can imagine my surprise. The Bible?

Yeah, the Bible, Dr. Eastern Europe said. The Bible contains some fundamental truths about human nature. Both the good and evil can understand humanity better by reading the Bible carefully, Dr. Eastern Europe told me.

And the Bible says that all human beings are sinful. All human beings are capable of sin. All human beings are capable of depravity. Dr. Eastern Europe encouraged me to hold on to this Biblical principle and use it for evil and not for good. There was money in that.

I could not help but marvel at how purely evil Dr. Eastern Europe was. Communism must have been a systematic program to desensitize, I thought. I could not imagine anyone in Democracy who had no moral compunction and such a disregard for the fundamental value of human rights and human dignity.

There was money in depravity, I often reminded myself in the training process. Dr. Eastern Europe was perfect to desensitize me of the morals learned in a Democratic society. Communism did one good thing – certainly for me. It brought me Dr. Eastern Europe and one step closer to becoming a wealthy man.

Dr. Eastern Europe explained that because all human beings are sinful or prone to sin, even a respectable woman is prone to sin. Sin is alluring to all and given the right chance and the right push, people will fall into the world of depravity and sin, Dr. Eastern Europe assured. Dr. Eastern

Europe said: Don't you just love the Bible?

Well, if I can use the Bible for wealth derived through depravity and sin, then the Bible is great! It pays to know the Bible.

Dr. Eastern Europe said that the best way to get the woman to beg for sex is to give her a good foreplay. Use your fingers to caress the woman's nipples and her vaginal area. She will experience the natural biological process of excitement. She will become sexually aroused. A woman's body is wired that way, Dr. Eastern Europe said.

When the woman is physically and sexually aroused, particularly beyond a certain point, then her body longs for sex. It is not only psychological, it is biological. The more aroused the woman is, the easier it is to get her to beg for sex. It doesn't matter how respectable the woman is.

Dr. Eastern Europe said another thing about the Bible. He told me to read Psalms 1. It says that you should not even sit with evil doers. Why? Because evil will become enticing.

What? Just sitting together with sinners will make sin enticing? It didn't make much sense at first, but fortunately, Dr. Eastern Europe explained things to me nicely.

You see, Dr. Eastern Europe elaborated, if people are prone to sin and that is basic human nature as taught in the Bible, then just sitting in a place of sin or with sinners will heighten their desire to sin. It is the case with all human beings, according to the Bible.

Yeah, it is theoretically possible that a righteous person sitting in a place of sin may overcome temptation, but it is far more difficult than not. His or her human nature will work and weaken the resolve not to sin. More often than not, just by being in the place of sin or with active sinners, one will be more prone to commit the sin. That is why Psalms 1 warns against places of sin and being with sinners.

Dr. Eastern Europe said that we could use it for evil advantage. Yeah, Psalms 1 was meant to warn Christians against sin and temptation, but we could use it in a flip-flop way to cause people to sin. In other words, Dr. Eastern Europe explained, we could try to bring people to places of sin and get righteous people to sit with active sinners. This was a way to get people to fall into sin. And there was money in doing this effectively.

In the context of getting a woman to beg for sex, the idea in Psalms 1 can be used. Whereas a woman, especially a respectable woman, would never think about begging for sex in a normal circumstance, if you get her into foreplay, in a sexual context, it becomes so much easier to get her to beg for sex. She is not only biologically aroused, she is psychologically aroused in the context of sex.

I remember Dr. Eastern Europe letting out many sinister Eastern

European laughter while he was talking about using – or misusing – the Bible for evil intent. But the thought of making a lot of money dulled my conscience. I don't think Dr. Eastern Europe had any conscience to speak of.

Dr. Eastern Europe said that the process of psychological manipulation to enslave a woman should not end there. There are other things that you can do to make a woman hate herself, feel humiliation and degradation, in order to make her into your sex slave.

Dr. Eastern Europe explained that another psychologically manipulative thing to do is to cheat on the woman who has given herself up to you with another woman. Dr. Eastern Europe said that it is important to do this after you have done things to make her feel a sense of self-degradation and humiliation. This could backfire if she doesn't hate herself sufficiently enough. She has to feel a complete lack of self-confidence for this to work.

But if the woman is hating herself and lacks any self-confidence – of course, because of what you have done to achieve that end – cheating on her with another woman will work deliciously, Dr. Eastern Europe enthused.

There are some important principles to remember, Dr. Eastern Europe emphasized. The woman you cheat with must be attractive looking. If you can't find an attractive woman to cheat on with you out of her own free volition, then buy an attractive woman. Yeah, buy her. It doesn't matter if she is a prostitute, an escort, or an attractive woman in the street whom you pay to render you services. The important thing is that she has to look attractive.

Why is this important? If you cheat on her with someone who is just absolutely ugly, then she will despise you and not herself. But if you cheat on her with someone who is very attractive, then she will despise herself. It is definitely worth the money and consider it financial investment in order to enslave a woman to you.

Of course, your primary target for the degeneration project should be a wealthy woman. That goes without saying, Dr. Eastern Europe said. If the woman is a wealthy woman, then all the efforts for psychological manipulation is worth it. It is a worthwhile investment to buy the attractive women to make the wealthy woman jealous and enslave her to you.

Dr. Eastern Europe said that cheating with an attractive woman will not only make the wealthy woman who has given herself to you jealous, it will make her desperate. She will feel a need to hold on to you. Thus, she will become blind and will spend whatever money she has to hold on to you. She may buy you an extravagant Christmas gift or a love token. She may be so disoriented that she may think that showering money on you and giving you expensive gifts will bind her to you.

Of course, you knew that there was this financial pay-off waiting for you after your hard work. Why else would you work so hard to enslave her to you? There is a lot of money in a project of psychological manipulation with a wealthy woman.

Dr. Eastern Europe explained that there is another thing that was important to remember. Dr. Eastern Europe said that it was important to give the woman hope – some sort of hope. Thus, any act of emotional cruelty must be coupled with some show of affection.

For instance, you can strategically play to have her see you with an attractive woman. She will feel jealousy and want to win you back. Show her that there is hope by buying her flowers or giving her some nice comment. When she feels that there is a hope of winning you back, she is prone to spend more money and shower more expensive gifts on you.

Dr. Eastern Europe reminded that psychological manipulation is just that – psychological manipulation. It involves artifice of much thinking, care for details, and brilliant execution.

It is important to focus on the money and wealth that are waiting at the end of the rainbow. It makes all the effort and energy spent and money invested worthwhile. After all, you have to spend money to make money, right? Hard work pays off, right? This is the case also with project of degeneration and sin meant to make money as in any other enterprise. Approach things like a businessman, like a manager in a company, Dr. Eastern Europe said.

Yeah, Dr. Eastern Europe opened my eyes to many things. He showed me things that I did not even know existed. Some may say that my naïve world was turned upside down. But I don't like to see it that way. Because the knowledge that I gained from Dr. Eastern Europe was sure to make me a lot of money, I consider my training under his tutelage invaluable and life-changing. Money is God, isn't it? Money talks. The world never listens to a moral man or a selfless man, when he has no cash. The world listens to a rich man. Money is the end all and be all of everything in this world we live in. For me, getting rich is the most important thing.

I am glad that Dr. Eastern Europe desensitized me to have the strength to enslave women without an ounce of conscience to keep me awake at nights. I am glad that I was trained to be ruthless and ruin people's lives at a whim. I exult in the fact that I was educated in the artifice of psychological manipulation that allows me to move people like pawns in a chess game. I am the king who will become wealthy in all this. I will use every chess piece, including the Queen.

Yeah, training in psychological manipulation was an important part of my training to make a lot of money out of depravity and sin. But it would not be complete without training in social deception. Dr. Eastern Europe, as polished as he was in psychological manipulation, would not have been

51

the best trainer for social deception. He's an Eastern European, for God's sakes! Yeah, you know what I mean.

For training in social deception, I turned to an Englishman. An English gentleman. To protect his identity, I will call him, Lord England. Who better than Lord England to train me in the art of social deception? After all, Lord England is from the English upper-crust society. He is nobility. He comes from a long line of nobles. He has been brought up in refinement. He understands upper-class society very well. He's a part of it. Since that's where the money is, he is the perfect trainer for social deception.

The first thing that Lord England taught me was that it was easy to deceive the English upper-class. This didn't seem to make sense at first. Aren't the people in the English upper-class highly educated and experienced in worldly affairs?

Yeah, that is true, but it is also true that the English upper-class live by a type of protocol that is easy to manipulate, Lord English said. I was all ears after that. If I were to understand social deception, I had to understand how upper-class social protocol could be breached to my advantage. Lord England was the right person to show me the flaws in the system. Lord England was the perfect trainer to help me fall through the cracks in the upper-class social system.

Lord England told me that it was important to understand the upper-class social protocol. Yeah, he was in the English society and guided by English upper-class social protocol, but every society, regardless of country or place has social protocol that the upper-class – or the wealth class – was guided by. Understanding the social protocol was crucial, Lord England said. If you understood the social protocol and abided – at least on the surface – by it, you could even get away with murder.

Yeah, you could imagine that my mouth was gaping open at this point. Perhaps, it's because I come from the working classes. Yeah, we have ways of doing things, but just because we followed the normative ways of doing things, we would not get away with murder. The working class, I came to realize, is far more moral than the upper-class. It was a revelation – a revolutionary revelation.

Lord England described what the important social protocols were. The most important thing to know was how to approach people. There were social protocols that guided how to start a conversation and continue a conversation. The best thing for me in my condition – he said – is not to talk to much. Just nod and give the other floor space. The more they talk and the more you nod, the more you ingratiate yourself to them.

Furthermore, Lord England said that I need to learn the artifice of flattery. All wealthy people like flattery. All upper-class people are vulnerable to flattery. If you learn to flatter the upper-class in just the right way, it will open doors. People will come to think well of you and even praise you. When upper-class individuals praise you and in a sense vouch for you, you get more credits to do your evil deed – you can get away with more, in other words.

Lord England explained that once you have upper-class individuals praising you in public, your future is guaranteed. Why would this be the case? – I thought. Just because a few wealthy individuals praise you, you have a license to do a lot of things? This didn't make sense to me. It doesn't work like that in the working class settings I am used to.

But that's precisely it, Lord England said. The working class seems simple on the surface but the working class operates more on an individual level and thinks in practical ways about everything. A part of the reason is that most working class people are working hard and they have to watch where their money is being spent. Everyday worries keep their feet on the ground.

They don't have the luxury or the space to let things slip past them.

The upper-class is different, Lord England explained. The upper-class does not have to worry about where every penny is going. The upper-class doesn't have to worry about half the things that the people in the working class have to worry about. The upper-class never really has to think about going hungry, not being able to take a vacation, not having enough money to educate their children, not buying new clothes every year, and having a lack of possessions. For the upper-class, it is a question of whether to buy a BMW or a Bentley. For the working class, it's a question of having enough money for transportation – any kind of transportation.

Because upper-class people do not worry about practical things in life, they tend to be very impractical and live in the clouds. Many of them lose touch with reality of life. The only thing that keeps them together is the social protocol that guides their upper-class society. That is why if you work within the protocol, you could even get away with murder.

When you flatter upper-class individuals effectively and they feel good about themselves, they will say good things about you. Once you get them to say positive things about you publicly, you got them hooked. Now, they have attached their name to their "recommendation" of you. Within the upper-class social protocol, it would look bad if they changed their public comments about you. They have, in effect, attached their good name to you.

If you follow protocol and get upper-class individuals to attach their good name to you, you can do no wrong – at least as they are concerned. Even if they despise what you do or even despise you for what you do afterwards, they will maintain their original public comments of praise, not for your sake for their own sake. They are concerned about their societal status in the context of their upper-class social protocol, Lord England explained.

Yeah, you could imagine how glad I was to hear all this. Putting in little time, I could manipulate the upper-class society like a puppeteer. Who would have thought that a sophisticated upper-class is so easy to manipulate. It suits me fine, of course. Lord England was helping me to learn effective social deception. It will make me money and lots of it. Upper-class society individuals will be suckers – my suckers – in my elaborate scheme to make me rich on depravity and sin. Once they give me their public endorsement, they will always have to endorse me, no matter how odious such an idea may appear to them. They are prisoners of their social protocol.

Lord England taught me another important thing. He said that if you have the social endorsement of upper-class individuals, you will be able to bed any upper-class woman. Upper-class women are easier to bed than working class women because they are living in the clouds and aren't concerned about practical things. In a sense, they are more superficial and "easy." As long as you follow the protocol of their class, you can get away with anything.

This revelation was just great, as you can well imagine. Since I was interested in making lots of money through my project of depravity and sin, it was welcome news to see that the upper-class social system where there is a lot of money is so easy to manipulate. Since my project of sin and depravity involved women and bedding women, I was even more excited to see that it was quite easy to bed upper-class women if you just follow social conventions and protocol of the upper-class.

Lord England explained that because upper-class women have grown up in protected environment, they do not have the defenses of working class women. Working class women have to put up with men at every turn. Upper-class women are generally left alone by men, many of whom are in the working class. Thus, life's experiences often make upper-class women more vulnerable for actual advances than working class women. As long as a man is able to penetrate the upper-class setting, it's quite easy to screw an upper-class woman. It's all about protocol and social location.

That certainly is not the case in the working class. You can penetrate the working class social system, you ain't gonna get some. Lord England actually taught me to disrespect upper-class women. I guess having disrespect for upper-class women is important because I was interested in making money off of them and from exploiting them. Lord England was the right person to give me the confidence to exploit the upper-class and milk it for all it's worth.

Lord England told me that it was important for me to surround myself with upper-class individuals. If I were able to get a private, boarding school education, then I should use it to connect to the "boys' network." Hang out with elite men and upper-class women will think that they could screw you because you are "in." Then, they will let their guards down, and you can go in for the kill.

The more you are seen with a group of elite individuals the easier it is to get upper-class women into bed.

An important step to capitalize on is to go out with one upper-class woman. If you can do this, then you can potentially go out with any upper-class woman. Manipulate the system strategically and with careful planning, Lord England told me.

I often wondered why Lord England was giving the secrets away. After all, I was not from the upper-class. I was from the working-class. But here he was giving away the secrets that could potentially undue his society as he knew it. I can ruin many women in his class and bring unhappiness to many families.

Then, it struck me. Lord England was too rich for his own good. This was just a game to him. Lord England was so bored with life that he treated life like a game. Working class people among whom I grew up never treated life like a game. It was a matter of life and death to toil and work day in and day out. But wealthy individuals like Lord England did not know what that meant. To Lord England and all like him, life was a big game.

In a sense, I was a part of that game. I was a working class individual who was being trained to be entered into the upper-class system to damage the people in the system. It made life – his boring aristocratic life – more interesting to have someone like me in the game. I wondered how many disaffected, bored aristocrat types were out there who also thought like him. They were so bored with life that they didn't care that someone like me destroyed their sisters, daughters, mothers, and aunts.

Yeah, to a working class guy like me the upper-class looked more and more screwed up with each passing day. That was just fine by me. I hated the upper-class anyhow. I just wanted to exploit the upper-class for all that it was worth and get rich doing it. If bored aristocrats like Lord England stupidly were willing to help me exploit his family and friends, I was not going to complain. I was just going to count the money and laugh at all the money that I made through my exploitation and program of degeneration and sin.

Yeah, Lord England was great because he not only taught me about upper-class social protocol and showed me how easy it is to exploit the upper-class, he actually helped me to develop a genuine disdain and disrespect for the upper-class. Whereas in the past, I looked up to people in the upper-class as being special, I now consider the upper-class as made up of self-important stupid individuals who allow themselves to be exploited without any coherent resistance. No self-respecting working class individuals would allow themselves to be exploited like that if they could help it.

Furthermore, and perhaps more importantly for my purposes, I came to disrespect upper-class women. Before, I thought of upper-class women as delicate flowers deserving respect. I thought of upper-class as intelligent and having self-respect. It's hard to disrespect a woman who respects herself. But I came to realize under Lord England's tutelage that upper-class women are far more stupid than working class women. Working class women respect themselves far more than upper-class women. You can't get a working class woman into your bed just because you are seen with a group of people. Those who have morals will not abandon them just because you are following a protocol.

Yeah, I found upper-class women petty and stupid. Lord England helped me to be ready psychologically and emotionally to exploit upper-class women and degrade them and make them hate themselves – all for my financial gain.

With the training I gained from Lord England, I was ready to practice social deception to enter into elite societies. With the training I gained from Dr. Eastern Europe, I was ready to exploit upper-class women for financial gain and profit.

I knew I was going to be a rich man. I knew as my training progressed. I knew as I talked with Dr. Eastern Europe and Lord England.

I was going to be very wealthy. My project of moral depravity and sin will make me wealthy. I knew what was possible – now, it was just a matter of doing it.

The Practice

Yeah, it is one thing to learn in a theoretical setting, it is a completely another thing to practice what you have learned in a real life situation. The practice requires adjustments and problem-solving that the theory does not necessarily require.

I believe that it was in practice that I proved myself to be brilliant. I used the training that I received and contextualized it in my context and in light of my life experiences and situation in life. I was brilliant in doing this and made tons of money already. There is money in moral depravity and sin. And it takes a brilliant individual like me to capitalize on it.

I will tell you one major way I contextualized my training. You see, I have a biggy thingy. Yeah, don't forget. I am Grandmaster Biggy Thingy Thai. I figure that my greatest asset is my biggy thingy. And I have learned to use it to my advantage.

I emphasize my biggy thingy at every turn. I try to encourage the myth that a big male genitalia is what gives women pleasure. Nothing is further from the medical truth. A big penis does not gratify a woman more than a smaller penis. Much of the physical excitement is done with outer areas of a woman's vagina.

But it is also true that sexual pleasure is more in the mind than not. If you can psychologically deceive a woman into thinking that a big penis gives more sexual pleasure, she may come to believe it. That belief may work to give her added pleasure. Half the sex is in the mind.

Having been trained in the artifice of psychological manipulation, I took my training a step further to add this dimension to my psychological manipulation.

Yeah, I don't hesitate to tell a woman that I have a big penis or to insinuate this fact. Then, I play mind games to entice her into having sex with me.

Surprisingly, I have found that women are psychologically weak. At least, they can be manipulated into having sex pretty easily. I use my big penis as a ploy and it works.

Sometimes, I take out my penis. It is pretty big and I have God to thank for it, I guess. But I ain't no Christian man – I am going to use my biggy thingy to make money and lots of it. I am a male prostitute, after all.

Yeah, I sometimes take out my biggy thingy and show it off. Yeah, I sometimes feel like a freak showing off an extra toe in a circus, but I try to push my sense of humiliation out of my mind. There is money at the end of the tunnel and just like the freaks showing off their oddities for pay, I do so accordingly.

Yeah, I even invite people to touch my biggy thingy. I meet women who have never seen such a big penis in real life, and they are curious. It's not too hard to get curious women to touch my biggy thingy.

Once they touch my biggy thingy, I have them hooked. I know that it is not too difficult to get them into bed from there. When they are touching my biggy thingy, it gives me the freedom to touch their breasts or their vagina. That gets them excited – it's a natural biological process. After a certain point, most women cannot resist.

I sometimes get women to do degrading things when I know that I have got them sufficiently excited sexually.

Yeah, Dr. Eastern Europe told me to do so in the context of a relationship, but you have to remember, I am a Thai male prostitute. I cater Dr. Eastern Europe's instructions to my context.

So, I entice innocent, unsuspecting women to have sex with me with my biggy thingy. They may hate themselves in the morning, but what does that matter? I get what I want. More importantly, I make lots of money in the process. I am a big Thai male prostitute.

What's great about getting the word out there about my biggy thingy is that it is like free publicity. People get all curious about my biggy thingy and I get more customers. I find that more often than not human sinful nature plays a role and many women become weak and want to try me out. That's fine by me since I am a Thai male prostitute and that's how I make my money.

But I learned my lessons well from Dr. Eastern Europe. There is little money in petty prostitution. As a Thai male prostitute, I will continue to serve the general female population with the goal of enriching myself, I know that there is greater money in – shall I say?– long-term investment.

This is where Dr. Eastern Europe's lessons on manipulating a relationship come in handy. And I have tried it out on rich women. It works. Coupled with my training from Lord England, I have been able to penetrate an upper-class setting. I have been given an expensive car as a gift and have been paid with cash.

Yeah, mama probably isn't proud of the way I make my money.

She's a God-fearing, church-going
Christian. I think she prays for me to
abandon my life as Grandmaster Biggy
Thingy Thai – the big Thai male
prostitute. But she lives in poverty. I
don't want to be like that. My God is
money and I will do whatever I have to
– however ruthless and however
immoral – to advance myself
financially.

Dr. Eastern Europe was
absolutely right. Women do become
vulnerable after they tell you that they
love you. You can do whatever you
want with them after that. You get
them to hate themselves by subjecting
them to degenerate things, and they
become like sex slaves to you. It's
amazing how that theory works.

I have tried with religious
women, respectable women, wealthy
women, politically powerful women,
and all other types, and it's worked in
many cases. Maybe I have done some
permanent psychological damage to
them, but that's all part of the game,
right? I am in this game to make lots

of money and I am accomplishing my vision and purpose. Yeah, I would call this my purpose in life. It's good to be rolling in doe.

Yeah, some of these women may never be able to have a normal relationship with a man or a trust a man ever, but is it really my fault? When I started to subject women to self-degradation and self-humiliation, they should have just left me, rather than showering me with gifts. They are responsible for what they did or what they did not do. They lost and I won.

Women are simpletons. They think that love will change me. I am Grandmaster Biggy Thingy Thai and all I want is to become wealthy. I will exploit any woman, any family, and any society to become wealthy. I feel no shame.

My conscience has been destroyed by the help of Dr. Eastern Europe and Lord England.

I will continue to use my biggy thingy to entice women into having sex with me. Now, I kinda enjoy the knowledge that they may hate themselves in the morning. I revel in the understanding that I am so powerful that I could get them to destroy their own lives and their important relationships. Call it the biggy thingy power. I am the Grandmaster Biggy Thingy Thai.

And like a good businessman, I am going to continue to exploit women and families for financial game. I have lots of plans for the future.

The Future

Yeah, the future looks bright for me. Who says there is no money in moral degeneration and sin? Yeah, historians say that moral degeneration and sin can destroy the social fabric of society. So what? What I care about is my life and in the short 100 years I am on earth, I want to live and make lots of money. I care about me, myself, and I. It's the survival of the fittest life out there. And I am fit to survive.

The women whom I exploit and use to get myself rich? Obviously, they are not fit to survive. If they are too stupid for me to exploit them, then they deserve to be like my slave. They are aiding in my project of moral degeneration and sin. More power to me!

I have quite a number of future projects lined up in my program of social degeneration and sin. Some projects are more open and others are – well, shall I say – more covert. I am a businessman – a brilliant businessman – to make a lot of money. My projects are to make money, plain and simple.

I will start telling you about my more open project. I figure that it would be a shame to let my conquests fade away in history. Some of the women that I have enslaved as my sex slaves are important people in society. Yeah, that's right. I have decided to exploit these women further and milk them beyond their grave, so-to-speak. How would I do that? By writing about the women who have been conquered, of course.

These simpleton women – what are they going to do about my further exploitation of them for my financial gain? They have paid up and then paid up some more as I exploited them right in front of their friends and family members. They have showered me with gifts and cash as I humiliated them and their families.

I will write a book about how I made intelligent women into my sex slaves and milked them for everything that they have got. Who's going to resist me? The feminists? Some of the women that I so expertly manipulated and exploited were feminist women. They allowed me to exploit them and degrade them.

Do you think that the families of the women that I have exploited will resist me? Some of them invited me into their homes and treated me like their guests. Do you think that they have the strength to resist me after I humiliated them in their own homes?

They would be too embarrassed to resist me. If I have learned my lessons from Lord England well, I know that they would be too embarrassed to resist me. After all, they have given me their praise and approval publicly by inviting me into their homes. Their friends and acquaintances will think that they are stupid to be so easily manipulated by me. They wouldn't want to humiliate themselves further – so they will think. Social protocol. It will protect me.

Yeah, I will exploit these women and their families further and get rich and fat off of the moral degeneration project. I will write all the sordid details. Yeah, it's something that I should be proud of, right? I used my training under Dr. Eastern Europe and Lord England effectively. They should be proud of the accomplishments of their star pupil.

Okay, now onto more covert projects to bring myself a lot of money and wealth.

This is the internet age after all, right? I am going to invest in some internet projects because I think that I will be able to make a lot of money off of it.

I will have an open internet website that would be like my personal/business website. It will tell a bit about me – well, just the bits that I want people to think about me. And it will also have some areas that they can pay to enter. They can pay to see some live webcam coverage. They will be able to download some short films of me in action.

Yeah, some of the film clips will be for pure entertainment and some of the clips will be kind of like how-to-guides. After all, I am good at what I do, however morally degenerate it is. I am sure that there will be people who would be interested in learning the artifice of the degenerate trade.

The trouble with Dr. Eastern Europe and Lord England is that they are purists. What I mean by that is that they actually believe in what they do – however twisted it may seem – as an art form.

I have no illusions. I am in this for the money. For me degeneration and sin are not something I do out of life philosophy or for the sake of art, but purely to make money. I am a businessman and I am brilliant at it.

Furthermore, I have contacts in the computer, web-business industry. So, I will use the web to make more money. I figure that if I do this right, I will make more money from the web project than anything else.

So, Dr. Eastern Europe and Lord England will be purist trainers. I will be a businessman. In the end, I will be far more famous and make far more money.

Dr. Eastern Europe and Lord England should be thankful that I will spread their philosophy and "art form" around the world through my how-to video clips on my website. I am popularizing their degenerate and sinful ideas for the masses. Yeah, God must hate me, but what is God even going to do when I have so much money?

Why confine myself to legit web business? There's good money to be made through illegal or shady type websites.

Here's an idea that I am working on. I will install web cams on my bedroom and have live feed. People will have to pay good money to enter these web areas, containing a type of snuff film feel. Unsuspecting women will be lured into it for manipulation and degeneration.

People will have to pay to view these live, snuff-type feeds.

What's more, I will add a gambling element to the website. Those who enter the snuff areas can place their bets on real-life situations.

They can bet to see if I will be successful in seducing a certain woman. They can bet to see if I will be successful in getting a woman to degrade herself in all kinds of ways. They can bet to see if I can corrupt a religious woman. They can bet on whether I can seduce someone's wife or a mother. They can bet on what kind of bad things I can get good people to do.

It will be a snuff area that will make me a lot of money. Yeah, most people would have moral objections to that kind of a website, but there is a lot of money in sin. People will be enticed by sin and depravity. The Bible is right about the alluring power of sin and depravity.

What I will do is capitalize on it and make myself incredibly rich.

People will pay good money — even their hard earned money — to see sin. They will pay even more to bet on sin.

Soon, I will have some spending their children's college funds to bet on my website. Who knows, if I'm good, I can get people to sell their houses and cars to gamble on my snuff website.

I am Grandmaster Biggy Thingy Thai and I have no morality or ethics. Only principle that I believe in is to make money and lots of it. I will use my biggy thingy to do that. I will ruin women, families, and societies to do that.

Sin sells. People pay for sin. More degenerate the sinful project, people will be enticed by it more. Yeah, it may destroy our society as we know it. But what do I care. I will be a wealthy man.

Sin is very powerful. And doesn't the Bible say that this world belongs to the devil until the big judgement day?

Well, I won't be around for the big judgement day. And if I am around, I intend to have enough money to pay off the judge.

For now, I just call me the child of the devil. I will capitalize on this world that belongs to the devil and bring more souls to him. In the process, I will make loads of money.

I do respect God – the Bible shows Him to be decent and just. But this world isn't. And it is in this imperfect world, I will manipulate what I have to make myself wealthy.

There is another project of degeneration that I would like to sponsor. Why confine myself to the internet world and do everything myself. I can open up a big global whorehouse.

My plan is to start by hiring a secretary who will serve as a whore and a secretary. Then, I will branch out and start a whole bandwagonful of prostitutes.

I figure, I have a ready market to turn to. I can go to Eastern Europe and hire Eastern European women for cheap. There are a lot of attractive

Eastern European women. Some have that innocent quality. Their only sin – in my opinion – is that they are poor.

I can exploit their poverty and use them and exploit them for my purposes. What would they get paid if they worked in their Eastern European country at an honest job? Like 50 dollars per month? I will offer them something far more than that and get them to work for me.

Yeah, I will make 1000 times more out of each of them than what I pay them. But they should be thankful that I have taken them out of their object poverty. If prostitution is good enough for me, it's good enough for them.

And it gives me a sick pleasure in seeing nice Catholic girls turned into my whores. It makes me feel good about myself. There is nothing sacred – not in religion or society. In such a setting, everything is possible. In such a society, I am actually a good man.

Money buys respect. I become a respectable man despite all the disrespectful things that I do.

Money is be all and end all. There is no one courageous enough to stand up to that.

My bandwagonful of prostitutes will follow me and we'll do world tours. Yeah, I will use my whores strategically to give them status. You know, the young impressionable types can easily be won over as I walk around with two beautiful blonde whores at my side. Being that they are from Eastern Europe and from poor but decent families will give them the feel of not looking like prostitutes but like the girl next door.

This all serves me well. My bandwagonful of wholesome looking whores will give me street credit and help me win over potential "business partners."

Am I a good businessman or what? All these projects of degeneration need planning and careful execution.

I probably have to hire some thug-types to protect myself. I may have to buy a gun for myself or learn martial arts. Maybe I'll work out as well.

It's a holistic project to enrich myself at the expense of social good and via exploitation of women.

From what I have already accomplished, I know how much degeneration is possible. I will build on that knowledge and expand my business.

Business tycoon, here I come!

The Trick

Yeah, the big trick in all this is to stay alive. To stay alive, I know I will need friends. I guess there are several ways to have friends. I guess I can buy some friends. After all, can't money buy everything?

What are friends? Friends often betray even their closest friends. This shows me that friends that I pay for are just as good as friends that I have whom I don't pay for.

In fact, I think that friends that you pay to be your friends are more dependable because you actually pay them. Friendship becomes a type of paid service.

Isn't that the way the wealthy operates? Aren't friends that the wealthy have all, in one sense or another, paid to be friends?

Since I am becoming one of the wealthy, I can start thinking along this line.

I will buy myself friends and then keep close tabs to see that they will be loyal friends.

Having loyal friends is the hardest thing. And I think that paid friends can be the most trustworthy and dependable.

Friends that you pay for are least likely to betray you because their livelihood will depend on you and your success.

So, just like my secretary will serve as my secretary and also to provide whore services, my friends will have duel purposes. They will be my friends and my employees.

Am I a good businessman or what? I am a big Thai male prostitute and I am proud of it, especially because I am becoming incredibly wealthy on account of it.

About the Author

Phlap Apirak a big Thai male prostitute and now a published author. Apirak takes pride in his ruthlessness with a sense of humor and half-hearted seriousness.

http://www.TheHermitKingdomPress.com